Table of Contents

Dedicated to Eva

Zen To Done

The Ultimate Simple Productivity System

by

Leo Babauta

Zen To Done

ISBN 1-4382584-8-8

Introduction

" Much of the stress that people feel doesn't come from having too much to do. It comes from not finishing what they've started."
David Allen

This book was written for those who want to get their lives organized and actually execute the things on their to-do list.

If you're one of those people, you'll find some valuable concepts in this book.

Zen To Done (ZTD) is a system that is at once simple, and powerful, and will help you develop the habits that keep all of your tasks and projects organized, that keep your workday simple and structured, that keep your desk and email inbox clean and clear, and that keep you doing what you need to do, without distractions.

That's a lot to ask of a little e-book. And in fact, this book won't do all of these things for you -- you have to do it. You have to really want to change your habits, but what's provided in this system are the tools for doing that.

And let me say that changing your habits are possible. Using the habit-changing techniques I describe in this book, and on my site, Zen Habits, I have made many habit changes: I quit smoking, started running, started eating healthier, completed a marathon, doubled my income and got my finances in order, became a vegan, have almost eliminated my debt now, completed a triathlon, lost more than 20 pounds, and started a successful blog, to name a few. So yes, habit changes are definitely possible, if you start small, find the right motivation, and maintain your focus.

I've also become more organized and productive. Only a couple of years ago, my desk was cluttered, I kept multiple lists of things that I
was always losing or forgetting about, I had a ton of things to do and was overwhelmed by the chaos and complexity of my day.

Email inbox was overflowing, and so were my physical inbox and voicemail inbox. I kept forgetting to do things, and in general was disorganized and unproductive.

But I began changing those habits, one by one. Today, my inboxes are all empty. My list of things to do today is a simple list of three very important things. I get them done. I am able to clear distractions and focus. I write things down, in one place, so I don't forget them.

My life is much more sane now, more simplified and more focused. I get a LOT more done -- from all the work in my day job, to writing the blog, to writing for six other blogs, to completing personal projects, and still having time for my family. I am happier and more productive, and it's all due to a few simple habit changes.

You can do this too, believe me. I'm no super-human -- I simply made the commitment to improve, and began changing my habits, one at a time.

Read on, and see how you can do these things too. Now, I don't expect you to adopt the entire system -- everyone works differently. That's the beauty of ZTD: you can choose those habits that work best for you.

Good luck, and enjoy this book. Changing your habits can be exciting, and I urge you to enjoy the journey.

Chapter 1:

Why ZTD?

"Simplicity is the ultimate sophistication." Leonardo DaVinci

I decided to take some of the best concepts from some of the best productivity systems ever invented, including, David Allen's Getting Things Done and Stephen Covey's 7 Habits of Successful People, add some other useful concepts, and distill them into a very simple and usable productivity system called Zen To Done (ZTD).

Why "Zen To Done"? Well, first off, the blog is called Zen Habits, and "Habits To Done" doesn't sound cool enough to me. I also thought of "Simple To Done" but the acronym didn't seem right. Second, ZTD captures the essential spirit of the new system: that of simplicity, of a focus on doing, in the here and now, instead of on planning and on the system.

If you've been having trouble with GTD, as great as it is, ZTD might be just for you. It focuses on the habit changes necessary for GTD, in a more practical way, and it focuses on doing, on simplifying, and on adding a simple structure. Read on for more.

ZTD attempts to address five problems that many people have with GTD. I should note that GTD isn't really flawed, and doesn't really need modification, but everyone is different, and ZTD is a way to customize it to better fit different personality types.

ZTD addresses five problems people have with GTD:

1) **GTD is a series of habit changes**. This is the main reason why people fall off the GTD system — it's a bunch of habit changes that are attempted all at once.

   As I talk about on my blog, Zen Habits, focusing on one habit at a time is best, and guarantees the most success. In addition, GTDers don't apply proven habit-change methods (the ones I talk about on Zen Habits) to change their habits.

   Solution: ZTD focuses on one habit at a time. You don't have to try to adopt the entire system at once — it's overwhelming and it's too hard to focus on your habit changes if you do too many at a time. Instead, focus on one at a time, and adopt the system in phases. Use proven habit-changing methods (30-day challenge, commitment, rewards, motivation hacks, etc.) to successfully adopt each new habit.

2) **GTD doesn't focus enough on doing.** While it's called Getting Things Done, often what we end up doing most of the time is Getting Things in Our Trusted System. The book, while presenting an excellent system, focuses more on the capturing and processing stages than it does on the actual doing stage.

   Solution: ZTD focuses more on doing — and how to actually complete your tasks, in a simple, stress-free manner.

3) **GTD is too unstructured for many people**. This can be one of the brilliant things about GTD — its lack of structure, its in-the-moment decision making about what to do next — but it can also be a huge source of confusion for many people. Some people need more structure in their day, and GTD can be disorienting. Different people have different styles.

   Solution: ZTD offers a couple of habits to address this: the plan habit, where you simply plan your three MITs for the day and your Big Rocks for the week, and the routine habit, where you set daily and weekly routines for yourself. These habits, like all the habits of ZTD, are optional. If they don't work for you, don't adopt them. But for many people, they will compliment the other great parts of GTD perfectly.

4) **GTD tries to do too much, which ends up stressing you out.** GTD doesn't discriminate among all the incoming stuff in your life, which again is part of its beauty. But the problem is that we put everything on our lists, and end up being overloaded. We try to do everything on our lists. This isn't really a problem with GTD, but a problem with how we implement it. But it should be addressed.

5) **Solution: ZTD focuses on simplifying.** Take as much stuff off your plate as possible, so you can focus on doing what's important, and doing it well.

6) **GTD doesn't focus enough on your goals.** GTD is purposely a bottom-up, runway-level system. While it does talk about higher levels, it doesn't really go into it much. As a result, GTD is more focused on doing whatever comes at you rather than doing what you

should be doing — the important stuff.

7) **Solution: ZTD, as mentioned above, asks you to identify the big things you want to do for the week and for the day**. Another habit in ZTD is for you to review your goals each week, as a way of staying focused on them throughout the year. GTD contains an element of this, but ZTD extends it. Again, GTD is a brilliant system, and works very well. But ZTD takes some of the problems that people have in implementing it, adds other powerful concepts, and adapts the system for real life.

Chapter 2:

Overview - What is it?

"The things that matter most should never be at the mercy of the things that matter least." Goethe

So let's take a look at what Zen To Done really is: it's a set of 10 habits that will help you get organized, simplify your life, get things under control, and actually get things done.

If you adopt ZTD, you are under no obligation to do all 10 habits ... you should pick the ones that will work for your individual style, and focus on mastering those.

Each of these habits should be learned and practiced one at a time if possible, or 2-3 at a time at the most. Focus on your habit change for 30 days, then move on to the next.

That can be difficult, I know, but in the long run the habits will stick better if you focus on them one or two at a time. And over the course of a year, you'll have mastered them all -- and I don't think becoming completely organized and productive in one year is such a bad accomplishment.

The order listed below is just a suggestion — you can adopt them in whatever order works best for you. Habits 1-8 are the most essential, but I suggest you give Habits 9-10 serious consideration too. I will expand on each of these 10 habits in the chapters to follow.

1. Collect

Habit: ubiquitous capture. Carry a small notebook (or whatever capture tool works for you) and write down any tasks, ideas, projects, or other information that pop into your head.

Get it out of your head and onto paper, so you don't forget it. ZTD asks you to pick a very simple, portable, easy-to-use tool for capture — a small notebook or small stack of index cards are preferred (but not mandated), simply because they are much easier to use and carry around than a PDA or notebook computer. The simpler the tools, the better. When you get back to your home or office, empty your notes into your to-do list.

2. Process

Habit: make quick decisions on things in your inbox, do not put them off. Letting stuff pile up is procrastinating on making decisions. Process your inboxes (email, physical, voicemail, notebook) at least once a day, and more frequently if needed. When you process, do it from the top down, making a decision on each item: do it (if it takes 2 minutes or less), trash it, delegate it, file it, or put it on your to-do list or calendar to do later.

3. Plan

Habit: set MITs for week, day. Each week, list the Big Rocks (most important tasks) that you want to accomplish for that week, and schedule them first. Each day, create a list of 1-3 MITs (basically your Big Rocks for the day) and be sure to accomplish them. Do your MITs early in the day to get them out of the way and to ensure that they get done.

4. Do

Habit: <u>do one task at a time, without distractions</u>. This is one of the most important habits in ZTD. You must select a task (preferably one of your MITs) and focus on it to the exclusion of all else. First, eliminate all distractions.

Shut off email, cell phone, Internet if possible (otherwise just close all unnecessary tabs), clutter on your desk (if you follow habit 2, this should be pretty easy). Then, set a timer if you like, or otherwise just focus on your task for as long as possible. Don't let yourself get distracted from it. If you get interrupted, write down any request or incoming tasks/info on your notepad, and get back to your task. Don't try to multi-task.

5. Simple Trusted System

Habit: <u>keep simple lists, check daily</u>. You can use context lists, such as @work, @phone, @home, @errands, @waiting, etc., if those work for you. ZTD suggests that you keep your lists as simple as possible. Don't create a complicated system, and don't keep trying out new tools. It's a waste of time, as fun as it is. Either use a simple notebook or index cards for your lists, or use the simplest list program possible. You don't need a planner or a PDA or Outlook or a complicated system of tags. Just one list for each context, and a projects list that you review either daily or weekly. Linking actions to both projects and contexts is nice, but can get too complicated. Keep it simple, and focus on what you have to do right now, not on playing with your system or your tools.

6. Organize

Habit: a place for everything. All incoming stuff goes in your inbox. From there, it goes on your context lists and an action folder, or in a file in your filing system, in your outbox if you're going to delegate
it, or in the trash. Put things where they belong, right away, instead of piling them up to sort later. This keeps your desk clear so you can focus on your work. Don't procrastinate — put things away.

7. Review

Habit: review your system & goals weekly. ZTD's weekly review asks you to do a quick check of your system, and also focuses on reviewing your goals each week. During your weekly review, you should go over each of your yearly goals, see what progress you made on them in the last week, and what action steps you're going to take to move them forward in the coming week. Once a month, set aside a little more time to do a monthly review of your goals, and every year, you should do a yearly review of your year's goals and your life's goals.

8. Simplify

Habit: reduce your goals & tasks to essentials. If you attempt to tackle all incoming tasks, you can quickly become overloaded, and be left without the necessary focus on the important tasks (MITs). So instead, ZTD asks you to review your task and project lists, and see if you can simplify them. Remove everything but the essential projects and tasks, so you can focus on them. Simplify your commitments, and your incoming information stream. Be sure that your projects and tasks line up with your yearly and life goals. Do this on a daily basis (briefly, on a small scale), during your weekly review, and your monthly review.

9. Routine

Habit: set and keep routines. If other productivity systems are too unstructured for you, try the habit of creating routines to see if it works better. A morning routine (for example) could include looking at your calendar, going over your context lists, setting your MITs for the day, exercising, processing email and inboxes, and doing your first MIT for the day.

An evening routine could include processing your email and inboxes (again), reviewing your day, writing in your journal, preparing for the next day.

Weekly routines could include an errands day, a laundry day, financial day, your weekly review, family day, etc. It's up to you — set your own routines, make them work for you.

10. Find your passion

Habit: seek work for which you're passionate. This could be your last habit, but at the same time your most important. GTD is great for managing the tasks in your life, and trying not to procrastinate on them. But if you're passionate about your work, you won't procrastinate — you'll love doing it, and want to do more. The habit to form here is to constantly seek things about which you're passionate, and to see if you can make a career out of them when you find them. Make your life's work something you're passionate about, not something you dread doing, and your task list will almost seem like a list of rewards.

Chapter 3:
Minimal ZTD — the simpler alternative

"Everything should be made as simple as possible, but not simpler." Albert Einstein

For some people, implementing 10 new habits, even if they're done one at a time, is overwhelming, and still too complicated. So for those who want to implement the simplest system possible, here's the minimalist version of ZTD — a way to be productive without all the fuss.

It's only four habits: collect, process, plan, and do. It also only uses two tools: a small notebook, and a pen.

1. **Collect**: Carry a small notebook and write down any tasks, ideas, projects, or other information that pop into your head. Get it out of your head and onto paper, so you don't forget it.

2. **Process**: make quick decisions on things in your inbox, do not put them off. Process your inboxes (email, physical, voicemail, notebook) at least once a day, and more frequently if needed.

3. **Plan**: set MITs for each week, and each day. Do your MITs early in the day to get them out of the way and to ensure that they get done.

4. **Do**: focus on one task at a time, without distractions. Eliminate all distractions, then just focus on your task for as long as possible.

Don't let yourself get distracted from it. Don't try to multi-task.

What the Minimal ZTD system leaves out

This version leaves out six habits: keeping a system of simple lists, organizing everything, weekly reviews, simplifying your tasks and projects, setting routines for yourself, and finding your passion.

While I think these six habits are valuable, they are not absolutely necessary for a minimalist system.

The Minimalist Implementation

So how do you implement this system, and what do you need? First the tools: A small notebook and a pen. That's all.

So here's how you implement the system:

1. Use your notebook to write everything down as you think of it. This allows you to get things off your mind and not forget them.

2. When you get to your desk or home, add those new tasks to your Master To-do List, which you can also keep in your notebook.

3. At the beginning of each day, review your list, and write down 1-3 MITs that you'd like to accomplish for the day.

That's your whole planning system. You don't need any more than that.

4. Get your MITs done as early as possible. When you do each task, clear away all distractions and focus on doing that one task only. Do not multi-task. When you're done, move on to the next MIT.

5. If you complete your MITs, go to your Master List and see what's the next most important task on the list. Do it as in Step 4 above. Repeat as needed.

You don't really need 10 different lists, and if you don't keep those different lists, you don't need a weekly review. I would still suggest you set a single goal for the year, and always focus on the next step needed to achieve that goal.

Also optional: add any of the habits that are left out of this minimalist system later, if you think they would help.

Chapter 4:
Forming the 10 Habits

" The beginning is half of every action." Greek Proverb

An essential part of ZTD is the forming of the 10 Habits, one at a time. One of the main problems people have with other productivity system, probably without knowing it, is that they are a series of habit changes that people attempt to undertake all at once.

They get enthusiastic about it, and try and do it all in one shot, and then fall off the wagon. They get back on, and then fall off again. It's almost like dieting or exercise — if you don't adopt successful habit change methods, you will keep failing and eventually get discouraged and quit.

Well, in my experience, habit changes aren't something to be taken lightly. They can be successful, but it takes a lot of energy and focus and motivation, and it's hard to do that with a bunch of habits all at once. I highly recommend that you start with one habit, and apply proven habit-change methodology to that habit, and then once that has become a habit, move on to the next habit.

Now, I understand that's not easy. When you take on a productivity system, you want to do it all at once. You're excited and enthusiastic! Trust me, I've been there. But take that excitement and channel it into one habit, and you will be hugely successful.

Doing one habit at a time will take some patience, but at

the same time it's not as overwhelming and it's much easier to adopt this way. For some people, becoming productive and organized can be overwhelming, and a major life change. I am an advocate of gradual life changes, ones that will last for a long time, not just for a few weeks.

If you are already good at some of these habits, and if you are good at changing your habits, it's possible to do more than one at a time. I wouldn't recommend more than 2-3 at a time, though, because the more you do, the less your chances of success.

If you are already good at ubiquitous capture, for example, you could try adopting it as a habit along with, say, processing your inboxes. But don't try to do much more than that. Start simple, and gradually add the other habits as you see fit.

Now, which habits should you adopt first? I recommend the order that they're listed in, but that's far from mandatory. You could easily do them in reverse or scramble them, or form an algorithm to decide. I suggest that if you don't want to do them in the recommended order, see which ones will benefit you the most, and give those a higher priority.

Rome wasn't built overnight, and you can't change from being undisciplined, unorganized, procrastinating, unproductive (as I once was — I'm not accusing you of being these things) to organized, productive, with a do-it-now habit. Give yourself time to make these changes. At the end of this year, if you start now and adopt 1-2 habits per month, you will have some great habits adopted.

Habit Change Methodology

What are the methods you can use to make these habit changes successful? Here are some of the most important:

1. **Commitment**. Commit yourself to your habit change, big time. Make your commitment as public as possible — put it on your blog, join an online forum and tell them about it, tell your family and friends, send out a daily email update on your progress. The more positive public pressure, the better.

2. **Practice**. Changing your habits is a skill, and like any skill, it takes practice. Commit yourself to a 30-day Challenge, and try to do your new habit every single day for 30 days. You will be training yourself to do that new habit, over and over. If you mess up, don't beat yourself up, but just try again. Practice makes perfect.

3. **Motivation**. Find as many ways to motivate yourself as possible. See the Top 20 Motivation Hacks.

4. **Tracking**. It's best if you log your progress on your habit every day. This may sound difficult, but it will make your habit change much more likely to be successful. Log it in before you go to bed, placing your log next to your bed. It'll motivate you, and will make you feel great as you look back on all your progress.

5. **Support**. Join an online group, or do your habit change with a partner. However you find it, get others to do a habit change with you, and it will be much easier.

6. **Rewards**. Reward yourself often, early on — at the end of each of the first three days, and then at the end of every week, and then a big one at the end of your 30-day Challenge.

7. **Focus**. It's extremely important that you maintain your focus on this new habit for the full 30 days. That's why it's hard to do more than one or two habits at a time — you can't maintain focus. Find ways to bring your focus back to your habit. Post up signs or posters around your desk or home. Send yourself email reminders. Put it on your desktop picture. However you do it, keep a laser focus!

8. **Positive thinking**. This is perhaps the most important element. If you tell yourself that you can do this, that you will do it, then you will. Squash all negative thoughts, and replace them with positive ones. You can do this! Read this article for more.

Chapter 5:
Habit 1: Collect

" Much of the stress that people feel doesn't come from having too much to do. It comes from not finishing what they've started."
David Allen

Too often ideas pop into our heads, mail comes into our homes, paperwork comes onto our desks, phone numbers and appointments are given to us while we're on the go ... and they disappear or are forgotten or are relegated to a dusty drawer, never to be seen again.

The problem is that we have no system for collecting all of the information and papers and emails coming into our lives, and keeping them organized in a systematic way.

To address that problem, we're going to try to have a place for everything coming into our lives, and get into the habit of writing things down immediately, instead of relying on our brains to keep track of it all. If we rely on our brains, it's overwhelming, and our brains have a habit of forgetting what we need when we need it.

The collection habit is simple: have a very few amount of places to collect information and papers, and stick to that system.

So, for papers coming to your desk, you should have one place to collect them: an inbox. Don't ever stuff a piece of paper in a drawer, put a Post-it somewhere on your desk, or stack some incoming mail anywhere but your inbox. That's your one place to collect things, and you need to stick with it.

You should also have an inbox for your home, to collect all incoming mail, papers from work or school, phone messages, stuff you bring in from your errands, receipts -- everything, actually. Now things will never get lost again.

For emails, try to only have one account (it prevents multiple inboxes and confusion). You might have a bunch of other inboxes you check every day, somewhere online, although you might not think of them as inboxes -- MySpace or Facebook accounts, forums, other places where you get messages. These are all inboxes, and you should keep track of them and handle them in the same way. The fewer you have, the better.

We'll get to how to process all these inboxes to empty in the next chapter, in the habit called "process". For now, just be conscious of your inboxes, and trying to keep all incoming papers in the physical inboxes on your desk and at home.

Your notebook

But we also need to look at a special kind of inbox -- your collection tool for your ideas, notes, information given to you on while you're on the road, tasks you remember you need to do, action items that come out of meetings. In short, everything that comes into your life that's not in a written or recorded form.

Up until now, you might have been relying on your mind to remember those things, and maybe you added them to a to-do list when you got back to your desk. Unfortunately, your mind is a faulty tool. It forgets things when we need them, and then thinks about them when we don't need them.

So instead, we're going to make it a habit to get things out of your mind, and into written form. Carry a small notebook (or whatever capture tool works for you) and write down any tasks, ideas, projects, or other information that pop into your head. Get it out of your head and onto paper, so you don't forget it.

When you're in a meeting and an action item comes up that you need to do later, write it down. When your boss calls you to ask you to work on a project, write it down. When someone gives you a phone number or email address at a social gathering, write it down. You get the idea.

ZTD asks you to pick a very simple, portable, easy-to-use tool for capture — a small notebook or small stack of index cards are preferred (but not mandated), simply because they are much easier to use and carry around than a PDA or notebook computer. When you get back to your home or office, empty your notes into your to-do list (a simple to-do list will work for now — context lists can come in a later habit).

A popular choice, but not necessary: the Moleskine. It's my collection tool of choice, simply because it's portable, durable, and aesthetically pleasing. I love writing in it. However, any small notebook will do, really. You might also try the Hipster PDA.

I recommend analogue (paper) over digital for this habit,

but if your PDA or smart phone works for you, go for it. The reason I think analogue works better is that it's much faster — for digital, you not only have to pull it out, but you have to turn it on, go to the right program, click on an entry, and then enter through your entry system. With analogue, you just pull out the notebook and pen and write. Either way works, but I think that the simpler and easier the tools, the more likely you are to use them. Do what works for you, though.

The key with this capture habit is to write things down right away, before you forget, and to empty out your notebook as soon as you get home or to work. Don't procrastinate with these two steps, or they will pile up and you will be less likely to do them. Stay on top of it!

Also, carry it around, everywhere. No matter what system you use, it

should be very easy to carry around, and easy to jot down ideas quickly. You need to carry it wherever you go, including to bed, in stores, if you're hospitalized, wherever.

This simple habit of collecting all the information that comes into your life into a tiny notebook (and in a few other inboxes) will greatly improve your organization and eventually your productivity. You will stop forgetting things, stop losing information, and always know where things are, all the time.

Chapter 6:
Habit 2: Process

" There is more to life than increasing its speed."
Gandhi

Once you've gotten into the habit of collecting things in a
few inboxes, including a small notebook (or other simple
capture tool) that you use to carry around with you
everywhere, the question remains: what do you do with all
the stuff once you've collected it?
You process it, making quick decisions on each item and
disposing of them until your inboxes are empty or
everything you captured on your notebook is processed.

Process to empty.

Letting stuff pile up is procrastinating on making
decisions. If you process your inboxes, making quick
decisions and putting things where they belong, things
don't pile up. Process your inboxes at least once a day,
and more frequently if needed.

First, minimize your inboxes. Every place you have to go
to check your messages or to read your incoming
information is an inbox, and the more you have, the harder
it is to manage everything. Cut the number of inboxes you
have down to the smallest number possible for you to still
function in the ways you need to.

List all the ways you receive information, evaluate each to
see if it gives you value, and find ways to combine or
eliminate inboxes. If something's not giving you value,

consider eliminating it from your life. See if you can go a week without missing it. For all the rest, see if you can combine multiple information streams into one inbox. For example, how many places in your home do incoming papers get placed? Have one inbox at home for all mail, papers from work,

school papers, phone notes, computer printouts, schedules, and more. Have four email services? See if you can forward them all to one service. The fewer inboxes you have, the better. Aim for 4-7 inboxes if possible.

Next, master your inboxes. This stage will sound familiar to my long-time readers, but it should be covered here: Don't allow your inboxes to overflow. This will create a huge backlog of stuff for you to go through, and it will definitely stress you out. Instead, become the master of your inboxes.

Check and process your inboxes once a day. For some inboxes, you may need to check more than once (I check my email every hour), but don't check constantly and obsessively. That just wastes your time and cuts into your productivity and real life. But don't check less than once a day, because otherwise you'll allow it to pile up. Piles are your enemy.

Here's how to process:

1. **Process it from the top down, making quick and immediate decisions**. Start with the top item in your inbox, and make an immediate decision. Don't skip over it or put it back in or delay the decision.

2. **Delete**. If you don't need it, trash it. Make this your

24

first choice.

3. **Delegate**. Are you the person who should be doing this? If not, send it to someone else and get it off your plate.

4. **Do it immediately**. If the task will take 2 minutes or less, just do it rather than adding it to your to-do list.

5. **Defer it for later**. If it will take more than 2 minutes, add it immediately to your to-do list to do later

6. **File it**. If it's just something you need for reference, file it immediately. Don't use a Miscellaneous or To Be Filed file — that's just putting off the decision. Don't let your things to be filed pile up — just file it right away.

7. **In all cases, don't leave the item in your inbox**. Delete or file it. Work your way down through each item until your inbox is empty. Note: if you have hundreds of items in your inbox, it might be good to toss them all into a folder to be processed later (and schedule a couple hours to do that), and then start this process with all new items from that point on.

8. **Repeat this process, to keep your inboxes empty**. If you've minimized the number of inboxes you have, this shouldn't be too hard. Celebrate when your inbox is empty! It's a wonderful feeling. Remember: Don't check them all day long — schedule your processing time — and definitely don't have instant notification on.

Chapter 7:
Habit 3: Plan

" Spend some time alone every day." **Dalai Lama**

So you have a list of things to do, and a whole brand new day staring at you. What do you do today?

The decisions you make about what to do each week, each day, each moment, add up to a process called workflow. In ZTD, I suggest that you take the unstructured, moment-to-moment workflow of GTD and shape it into an optimal structure.

Why should you add structure and plan out your day and your week? Because otherwise you are too much at the mercy of the winds of change, reacting to what comes your way instead of deciding what's important and what you really want to accomplish. Take control of your day, instead of letting the needs and wants and priorities of others control it for you.

Now, each person has a different working style, and if structure isn't for you, I suggest you try the moment-to-moment style of GTD. It's not a bad way to go at all.

However, here's the recommended workflow of ZTD:

Each week, list the Big Rocks that you want to accomplish, and schedule them first (more on that in a moment). Each day, create a list of 1-3 Most Important Tasks (MITs -- basically your Big Rocks for the day) and be sure to accomplish them. Do your MITs early in the day to get them out of the way and to ensure that they get done.

This is one of the simplest of the ZTD habits, but also one of the

most important. Why? Because it gives purpose to your day and week. Instead of just trying to crank out a bunch of tasks on your to-do list, you are trying to do the most important ones.

Sure, you'll also do other tasks on your list, but you're identifying the ones that you really want to accomplish — the ones where you can look back on your day and feel proud of accomplishing something. Often we work hard and do a lot, but when we look back on our day, we haven't really accomplished anything.

So how do you do this habit? Here are some tips:

1. **Big Rocks**. At the beginning of each week (either Sunday or Monday, you choose), sit down and look at your to-do list. What do you want to accomplish this week? These are your "Big Rocks". The term comes from Stephen Covey's "7 Habits of Highly Effective People".

   It means that you should put the Big Rocks in your schedule first, and let the smaller rocks and gravel fill in the schedule around the Big Rocks -- otherwise, if you put the small rocks and gravel in first, they will fill up the schedule, leaving no room for the Big Rocks. Try to keep your Big Rocks to just 4-6 accomplishments per week, at first — later, as you get a feel for what you can accomplish, you might be able to add more. Try to be sure to include at least a couple of tasks to further along your yearly goals.

2. **Schedule**. Now take these "Big Rocks" and place them in your weekly schedule. Place only one or two per day, so you aren't overwhelmed.

   Place them in 1-2 hour blocks, early in the day if possible. Now that these important tasks are blocked out, you can schedule other stuff around them whenever necessary — but these are already there.

3. **MITs**. Each morning, decide what your Most Important Tasks are for that day. These will probably be the same as your Big Rocks for the day, although as things change you might have different MITs. Choose about 3 MITs for the day — this could include a Big Rock and a couple other important tasks. Block out time for them early in the day if possible — if you put them later in the day, other things pop up that will get in the way.

4. **Complete them**. Now here's the most important part: get them done. First thing in the morning, before you even check email, get that first MIT done. Clear away all distractions, and be sure to focus on only that task until it's done. When you're done, reward yourself … but be sure to move on to your next MIT shortly!

6. **Look back and say ahh**. If you complete your MITs, you will feel great. Be sure to look back on what you've accomplished and pat yourself on the back — or even reward yourself.

Chapter 8:
Habit 4: Do

" Talk doesn't cook rice." Chinese Proverb

The "Habit of Do" is the key to the ZTD system. It's the habit that's missing from many other productivity system, and yet it's the most important. All the rest is just busy work if you don't actually do the things on your to-do list.

Emphasize the doing above the system, the tools, the planning, the to-do lists.

ZTD focuses on doing your tasks one at a time, to the exclusion of all else. Don't multi-task, and don't let yourself get interrupted. Too often during the day we are checking our email, answering phone calls, talking to people as they come to our desk – all to the detriment of the task we're supposed to be doing.

The result? Things don't actually get done. Single-tasking and focus are the keys to execution. Here are some tips for finding focus and actually doing things on your list:

1. **Choose a Big Rock**. First, select a task (preferably one of your MITs) and decide that you are going to work on it either until it's done, or for a set amount of time (say 30 minutes).

2. **Get zoned**. Before you get started, eliminate all distractions. Shut off email, cell phone, Internet if possible (otherwise just close all unnecessary tabs), clutter on your desk, anything that might interrupt you.

3. **Timed burst**. Set a timer if you like (a simple one like CoolTimer will do), or otherwise just focus on your task for as long as possible. Don't let yourself get distracted from it.

4. **Interruptions**. If you get interrupted, write down any request or incoming tasks/info on your notepad, or toss the document into your inbox, and get back to your task. Don't try to multi-task.

5. If you feel the urge to check your email or switch to another task, stop yourself. **Breathe deeply**. **Re-focus yourself**. Get back to the task at hand.

6. **The inevitable**. There are times when an interruption is so urgent that you cannot put it off until you're done with the task at hand. In that case, try to make a note of where you are (writing down notes if you have time) with the task at hand, and put all the documents or notes for that task together and aside (perhaps in an "action" folder or project folder). Then, when you come back to that task, you can pull out your folder and look at your notes to see where you left off.

7. **Relax**. Take deep breaths, stretch, and take breaks now and then. Enjoy life. Go outside, and appreciate nature. Keep yourself sane.

8. **Ahhhh**. When you're done, congratulate yourself! Reward yourself with a short burst of email or blogs — but limit it to 10 minutes, and then move on to your next task. Don't let yourself get carried away — it's very easy to get off track and wander for hours.

Fixing execution problems

Now, if you do these things, and you're still finding resistance to doing the things on your list, here are some things you can do:

- **Tiny chunk**. Tell yourself you only have to do 5 minutes of work on it. That small amount of work is less intimidating.

- **Just start**. Once you get going, it's much easier to keep going. So tell yourself that all you have to do is start. I like to compare this to my philosophy of running: instead of worrying about having to do the whole run, I tell myself that I just have to lace up my shoes and get out the door. After that, it's really easy. Do the same thing with any task — just fire up your program, and do the first few actions (i.e. start typing). It gets easier after that point.

- **Reward yourself**. Don't let yourself check email (or whatever reward works for you — something that you need to do every day) until you do at least 10 minutes (or 15 or 20, it doesn't matter) on the task. Set a timer. Once your 10 minutes is up, set another timer for 5 minutes and do email. Then repeat.

- **Get excited about it**. This is actually a tip that helps with any of these points. If you are excited about doing something, you will not hesitate to do it. For example, I loved this topic suggestion, and I was excited about writing it. As soon as I had the chance, I sat down to write it and only took one break. But how do you get excited about a task? Try to find something exciting about it. Will it bring you revenue? What can you do with that revenue? Will it bring you new clients, new opportunities, new recognition? If you can't find anything exciting about a task, consider whether it's really important or not — and if not, find a way to not do it. Sometimes eliminating (or delegating or delaying) the task is the best option.

- **Stop focusing on negative aspects**. You might be focusing on how hard something is, or on all the obstacles. Try looking at the positive aspects instead. Focus on what a great opportunity this project represents ... an opportunity to learn, to get better at something, to make more money, to work on a relationship, to gain some long-term recognition, to improve your advancement opportunities. This is similar to the "get excited about it" item in the previous section. If you look at the opportunities, not the problems, you will be less terrified and more likely to want to do it.

- **Commit thyself**. If motivation is your problem, commit yourself to making some progress with a goal or project today, or every day this week — tell all your family and friends, write it in your blog, or join the Zen Habits forum — it's a great motivator. Then hold yourself accountable by reporting to others what you did today.

Chapter 9:
Habit 5: Simple, Trusted System

"Simplify, simplify, simplify." Thoreau

One of the keys to any time-management system is the to-do list -- it keeps all the tasks that you can't do at this moment organized so that you know what you need to do at all times.

David Allen's GTD asks you to separate your tasks into separate to-do lists, known as "context lists", such as @work, @ computer, @home, @calls, @errands, and so forth. The reasons is so that when you're in a particular context, you only have to look at the tasks you can actually do at this moment, rather than looking at a long list of tasks that are mostly un-doable right now.

In ZTD, it is important to keep a simple system that you will actually use ... a system that you will trust to keep your information. Here are the three components of a simple, trusted system:

1. **Setup**. A simple system would consist of inboxes, a calendar, lists, and a reference system.

2. **Tools**. It is also important that you use very simple tools, so that the system does not need to be maintained much.

3. **Usage**. Finally, the important thing is that you actually use the system, and make a habit of checking it daily.

The Setup

ZTD says that you should use the lists you need, but keep your system as simple as possible. While the concept of context lists are useful, they can be difficult to maintain. Instead, keep as few as

possible. A sample setup might look like this:

@work: for everything work-related.

@personal: all your personal tasks.

@errands: so you can have an easy errand list.

@calls: for calls you can make from anywhere.

@waiting for: a useful list for stuff you need to follow up on.

Someday/maybe: a list of stuff you don't want to or can't do right now, but want to check on later.

However you do it, remember that these are not your daily to-do lists. The work and personal lists are just master lists that you can pull from for your daily MITs and your Big Rocks (see Chapter 7). The errands, calls and waiting-for lists can be checked as needed, of course. In addition, if it helps, you could use a Project list, to keep track of your projects.

The other components of a system, besides the lists, would be inboxes (see Chapter 5), a calendar, and a simple filing system.

The Tools

And while many popular GTD tools (Kinkless, stikkit, Outlook, Remember the Milk, etc.) make things a bit complicated, the truth is that all you need are lists.

Many people get too caught up in fiddling with the tools, with creating complicated systems, changing tools and systems every week or two, instead of actually getting things done. But ZTD asks you to use the simplest tools possible, and then forget about them. ZTD is about the doing, not the tools.

So the obvious question is: which tool to use to keep your lists? Here are my recommendations — the simplest, most effective GTD tools:

- **Simple GTD**: This is my favorite, and the one I use right now. I was using Tracks, which is also simple and very good, but I recently switched because I wanted something a little simpler. Simple GTD has what you need, with a nice interface, but none of the frills. Play around with it — the interface is extremely intuitive and doesn't require a manual. It doesn't have a lot of features, but that's its appeal.

- **Moleskine**: Another of my favorites. Actually, any small notebook that fits in your pocket will do — the easy of use of a notebook (you don't have to power it up or press any buttons!) is perfect for this daily GTD habit. But the Moleskine has a special appeal — it is aesthetically pleasing, and wonderful to use. I highly recommend it!

- **Hipster PDA**: Popular among the low-fi GTD crowd,

the Hipster PDA is as basic as it gets, and extremely portable as well. Basically, it's a stack of index cards attached with a clip. You can find templates for printing them online, or just simply write your lists on them. The cool thing: you can toss the cards when they're full, and replenish your PDA at any time.

- **Tadalist**: Perhaps the simplest tool of them all, tadalist is simply a list program. No frills, although the interface is nice (it's from the same folks as Backpack and Basecamp). Create as many lists as you need, print them if necessary, check only the context you need. Simplicity at its best.

- **Todoist**: Another simple, slick to-do list manager, this has a few extra features, but nothing complicated. I don't use it simply because I don't like the outline interface, but that may appeal to some of you more. It's worth a look, at least.

Once you've selected a tool, set up your lists, and keep them simple! Other tools for a simple setup:

- **Calendar**: I suggest Google Calendar, 30 Boxes, Outlook or a paper calendar.

- **Reference system**: For paper filing, use manila folders in alphabetical order in a single drawer is a simple setup that works best. Just create a file for each project, client, and/or topic. For digital files, you could use a simple folder system similar to the paper one, or just archive stuff and search for them when you need them.

Usage

The next part of this habit, and really the most important part (more important than the tool you use), is checking your lists every day.

I suggest making it a part of your daily routine (more on this in Chapter 13), where you check your lists in the morning and at the end of the day, and of course check your calls and errands lists when you need them. This isn't such a hard habit, but it's one that you should give special focus for about 30 days. Because once you make checking your lists a daily habit, your life will become much more organized and productive.

Chapter 10:
Habit 6: Organize

" The best way you can predict your future is to create it." Stephen Covey

One of the oldest organizing truisms around, but perhaps the most important of all: "a place for everything, and everything in its place".
Why is it so popular? Because it works. Let's take a look at how to form this habit and never lose a thing again.

Are there papers scattered all over your desk? Do you look for your car keys every day? Do you know, at this moment, where every single thing in your life is?

Your life can be completely organized with one single rule: put everything in its home. It's a habit I'm trying to teach to my kids, so I don't have to keep picking up after them all the time, and because it's one of the most useful habits I've ever formed.

Here's how to do it:

- **Have a system**. Put all incoming papers in your inbox (at work and home). Process that inbox, either doing the tasks, putting them on a to-do list (and in an action folder), filing them, forwarding them, or trashing them. With this system, there's never any question as to what to do — you've got a limited set of options.

- **Find a home**: If you're about to put something down on your countertop, or table, or desk, or toss it on your couch or bed, think about this: is that where it belongs? Where is it's home? If it doesn't already have a home, find one. Designate a spot for that item or type of item. Car keys? Have one place where you put the keys, all the time. Dirty clothes? They don't go on your bed. Handcuffs? Put them in that special box in your closet marked "Taxes".

- **Simple filing system**: Once you've processed papers out of your inbox, you'll need a place to put them if you need to reference them later. Don't have a bunch of files stacked somewhere — create a simple filing system (alphabetical is easiest, although you could sort by hexadecimal instead if you're a geek). Always have blank labels and folders on hand so you can quickly make a new file if needed, and don't be afraid to make new files. Never have a Miscellaneous file. You might as well call it the Procrastination file.

- **Put it away immediately**. Yes, I know, you were going to put it away later. It's just sitting there until you can get to it. Well, after awhile, "later" creates piles and messes. Don't wait until later. Do it now!

- **Make it a habit**. Putting things where they belong is not something that's going to happen overnight. You'll forget, or get lazy. To really make it stick, you need to focus on that habit for 30 days. Do a 30-day challenge, concentrating your energy on it until it becomes automatic.

- **Pay attention to transitions**. The time between when you're doing one thing and when you're doing the next thing is a transition. This is the time when you should put stuff away where it belongs and clean up your mess, but it's also a time when we're not thinking about that stuff and only thinking about what we're going to do next (or the next episode of Gilmore Girls). While you're working on your Everything In Its Place habit, pay close attention to transitions. Awareness of these transitions will make it easier to remember to put things away.

- **Keep flat surfaces clear**. Never toss something on a countertop, table, desktop, bed, dresser top, coffee table, or the floor. If you do, catch yourself, and find another home for it. In fact, while you're at it, clear off all these flat surfaces, tossing half the stuff and finding homes for the rest. Ahhh! Isn't that nice? Who knew there was a desk under there?

- **Label**. These are the organizer's best friend. Have a label maker on hand, or at least some blank labels, and label containers or boxes, so you know the home of everything. I tried labeling my wife and kids but they didn't take well to it.

- **Evaluate**. Every now and then, it's good to review your organization of everything. Sometimes, it doesn't make sense to have something in one room when you usually use it in another. Sometimes, it's good to get three pairs of scissors if you use them frequently in three different rooms. Sometimes you need to declutter or re-organize a drawer or closet. Revisiting these things periodically will help keep things together.

If you ever lose a thing again, go back to the above tips, and work on them some more. If you never lose a thing again, think about how much time and money you've saved. If that happens, feel free to send me a check.

Chapter 11:
Habit 7: Review

" Besides the noble art of getting things done, there is a noble art of leaving things undone. The wisdom of life consists in the elimination of the nonessentials. "
Lin Yutang

Let's face it: even the best of us loses track of things over time, and loses focus on our goals, and let's the best-planned system fall apart a little. With a busy workweek, and a busy life outside of work, the best systems tend to gravitate toward chaos.

That's where the Weekly Review comes in — it gives you a chance to get things together and refocus yourself on what's important.
But in this chapter we're going to look at how to tap into the power of the Weekly Review in as little time as possible — the Simplified Weekly Review.

The focus of the Simplified Weekly Review is on reviewing your goals each week. During your weekly review, you should go over your single yearly goal, see what progress you made on it in the last week, and what action steps you're going to take to move it forward in the coming week.

Here's how to do a powerful weekly review in five simple steps:

1. **Review your single long-term goal, and short-term goal**. Review your life goals (if you haven't written

them yet, take some time to do it now), and from those goals, you should choose one long-term goal that you want to accomplish this year.

Just one goal, to allow you to focus on that goal completely. Only choose one — if you choose too many, you will lose focus,

and focus is the most important component in achieving a goal. Then choose one short-term goal that you can accomplish in the next week or so that will move you closer to your long-term goal. Once you've done this, every week's Weekly Review should be just a review of the progress you've made on that single goal, and a refocusing on that goal. It's important to refocus yourself on your goal every week, as this will keep you on track, keep your attention and energy where it should be, and continue to move you forward on your goal. (10-15 minutes in your initial planning session; 5 minutes every week thereafter)

2. **Review your notes**. If you've been following ZTD Habit 1 (Collection), you will have notes from the past week. Many of the tasks in your notes will be already done, but it's important to look back over them so you can find unfinished tasks, phone numbers to enter into your contacts, etc. Just do a quick scan and jot down any unfinished items. (5-10 minutes)

3. **Review your calendar**. Look back over your last week's calendar items to see if there's anything that needs to be moved forward, and to see if there's anything that triggers new tasks that need to be done. Also look over your upcoming week's calendar to see

if there's any tasks that need to be done. (5 minutes)

4. **Review your lists**. Whether you have multiple context lists or one to-do list, it's important to look over them, to make sure they're up-to-date. Cross off completed items. Also review your follow-up list, your someday/maybe list, and your project list, if you keep them. (10 minutes)

5. **Set your short-term goal this week and plan your Big Rocks**. In Step 1 above, if you've accomplished your short-term goal, you'll need to set a new one. If not, refocus yourself on that short-term goal, and see what mini-tasks you can do to complete it. List those tasks and any other really important tasks that you want to accomplish this week, and schedule them on your calendar. Put them early in the morning. These tasks should have the highest priority each day. Only put one or two on each day's schedule. (5-10 minutes)

Total time for review: 30 minutes, if you stay focused.

Don't get distracted, and go through each step quickly. You'll want to clear away all distractions, turn off email and the Internet (unless your lists and calendar are online), turn off your phone. At the most, these steps should take you 45 minutes.

By doing these essential tasks at your Weekly Review, you will not only keep your system together, but you will keep yourself focused on your goals.

Remember: just focus on one goal at a time, making it much more likely that you'll achieve it. Print it out and post it up if necessary. Send yourself email reminders. Tell everyone about it. Put it on your blog. However you do it, maintain that laser focus, and it will happen.

Chapter 12:
Habit 8: Simplify

" Before enlightenment, I chopped wood and carried water; after enlightenment, I chopped wood and carried water." Zen Saying

If you're like me, you have a long list of tasks to do, perhaps broken down by different contexts (work, personal, errands, calls, etc.). Your list of tasks is so long that it's overwhelming. You can never completely wipe out your list because it's growing every day.

Simplify your list down to the barest of essentials, and you can eliminate the need for complex planning systems.

The long to-do lists are one of the problems of most productivity systems. But the tasks on these lists have no priorities, and everything is added to your lists. In the end, it's overwhelming, and you are left extremely busy, trying to knock off all your tasks.

In this chapter we'll look at ways to reduce your goals and tasks to the essentials.

Let's first imagine the ideal scenario. Recently I've begun simplifying my time management system from GTD down to basically nothing. I still have long lists of things to do, but I don't look at them much anymore. Instead, I've begun the process of elimination, and focusing on what's really important.

Now my to-do list is basically one list of three essential

things I want to do today (my MITs). I also have a list of a few smaller tasks that I want to knock out, all at once, usually in about 30 minutes or so, leaving the rest of my day free for the more important tasks. I still use my calendar, just as a way of reminding me of appointments, but it's not really a time management tool. I don't need time management tools anymore — I've simplified my list down to three tasks, every day.

How can you get to this point? Here are the key steps:

- **Eliminate, eliminate**. Take a few minutes to review your task and project lists, and see how much you can simplify them. Make it a challenge. See if you can cut it in half! If you've got 50 items, cut it down to 25. Then try to cut it even further a few days later. How do you eliminate tasks? Sometimes a task gets old and isn't necessary anymore. Cross those out. Sometimes a task can be delegated. Do that, and cross it out. Read on for more tips.

- **Know what's essential**. How do you know what's essential? By knowing what your main goal is, and other goals if necessary. You really should focus on one goal at a time, but if you want to do 2 or 3, that's OK too. Just don't do 10 goals or anything. Those goals should be your essential projects. Any smaller tasks are essential if they help you accomplish those goals, and not essential if they're not related.

- **Simplify your commitments**. How many projects are you committed to? How many extracurricular stuff do you do? You can't do it all. You need to learn to say no, and value your time. And if you've already said yes, it's still possible to say no. Just be honest with people and tell them that you have a high number of urgent projects to complete and cannot commit to this any longer. Slowly, you can eliminate your commitments to a very small number — only have those commitments in your life that really give you joy and value.

- **Simplify your information stream**. I've recently gone through the process of eliminating most of my RSS feeds. I also have cut back on the number of emails I respond to. And for more than a year now, I haven't read a single newspaper, watched television (except DVDs), or read a single magazine. The news no longer gives me any value. Simplify the inputs into your life, and you can simplify the outputs.

- **Review weekly**. Your to-do list tends to build up over the course of a week. Take a few minutes each week to eliminate, and eliminate some more. You don't need a huge to-do list to be productive — just do the stuff that matters.

- **Big Rocks**. During your weekly review, figure out the most important tasks that you'd like to accomplish over the next week. Those are your Big Rocks. Now place them on your schedule, first thing in the day, on different days of the upcoming week. Make those the most important tasks each day, and do them first — don't let them be pushed back to the end of the day.

- **Biggest value**. Consider the case of two newspaper writers. One is super busy and writes a dozen articles a week. They're all decent articles, but they're pretty routine in nature. The second writer writes one article this week, but it gets the front page headline, it's talked about all around town and blogged about on the Internet, it gets him a journalism award and he becomes a big name in journalism. From this article, he lands a bigger job and a book deal.

That example is a bit extreme, but it illustrates the point that some tasks really pay off in the long term, and others just keep you busy and in the long run, don't matter at all. The first writer could have stayed home all week and slept, and it wouldn't have changed his world much (except he wouldn't get paid for that week). Focus on those big tasks, that will make a name for you, that will generate long-term income, that will give you lasting satisfaction and happiness. Those are your Big Rocks. Eliminate the rest.

- **Three MITs**. Here's your planning system each day: write down your three Most Important Tasks on a sheet of paper (I write mine in a Moleskine pocket notebook). That's it. Check off those tasks when you finish them. Devote your entire day, if possible, to those three tasks, or at the very least devote the first half of your day to them. Your MITs are basically the Big Rocks you planned for this week, and any other MIT that you need to do for today.

- **Batch small tasks**. During the course of the day, other stuff will come up that you really need to take care of or they could create problems for you later. Write those down on another small list of small tasks (mine is at the bottom of my pocket notebook page). You don't need to do them right now, most likely. Just write them down for later. Set a time (probably 30 minutes or so) to batch process these tasks sometime later in the day (perhaps 4 p.m.). Do your MITs first, and then do all the small tasks at the same time. These might be calls, emails, writing a short letter, doing paperwork, etc. Try to do them quickly and knock them off your list. You might have a few tasks left at the end of the day. Better to leave the small tasks until tomorrow than the big ones. Batch process email, too — if you do it throughout the day, it's just a bunch of interruptions. Just do it once or twice a day.

Chapter 13:
Habit 9: Set Routines

" Zen is not some kind of excitement, but concentration on our usual everyday routine." Shunryu Suzuki

Create weekly and daily routines to give your day and your week a more ordered and calm feeling.

Routines can also greatly simplify your work day and personal life, as your day won't be overly chaotic and complicated, you can group similar tasks together and batch process them, and you can be sure of doing the things you really need to do.

Most importantly, it puts you in control of your day, instead of putting you at the mercy of the ebb and flow of all incoming requests. Without a routine, we have no good way of saying "no" to requests as they come in, and we are at the beck and call of every person who wants our time and every website that wants our attention. That's not a good thing, not if you want to get the important things done.

Take control of your life. Set some routines and learn to follow them.

Here are some tips for doing that:

- **Work tasks**. Make a list of all the things you want or need to accomplish in your work life. This could be big things like the Weekly Review, or little things like paperwork or reports, or clearing your physical inbox each day, setting your MITs at the beginning of each day, reviewing your goals, communicating your progress with your boss, processing your email inbox to empty, phone calls, writing, designing, etc.

- **Personal tasks**. Do the same thing with your personal life. This could include things like exercise, yoga, meditation, writing in a journal, reading, reading your RSS feeds, as well as chores and errands such as paying bills, balancing your checkbook, laundry, cleaning routines, grocery shopping, pet chores, stuff in your kids' lives, going to the bank, going to the post office, fixing your kids' lunch, etc.

- **Batch process**. Take a look at your lists and find ways to put smaller tasks together. This saves time and cuts down on interruption. For example, if you have grocery shopping, going to the bank, going to the post office and going to the pet store on your list, put them together as "errands" and do them on one day.

- **Desk Day**. You can do a "desk day" each week for personal stuff and take care of processing your mail, paying bills, balancing your checkbook, filing personal papers, getting stuff ready for the post office, setting your weekly dinner menu and creating a grocery list. For work, you could batch process all phone calls into one hour, batch process email into one one-hour period, batch process paperwork, etc.

- **Daily list**. Now look at your lists and see which

ones need to be done every day. Those might include email, phone calls, setting your MITs, writing in a journal, exercise, reading RSS feeds, processing your physical inbox, and more. Plan out your daily routine. Don't schedule every minute of your day, but have certain set times each day when you do these daily tasks.

My suggestion is to have a morning routine (maybe one morning routine at home and another when you first get into work) and an end-of-the-day routine (again, for the end of your work day and for right before you go to bed).Leave the middle of the day (the biggest portion of the day) open for completing your MITs and other things that come up.

- **Weekly list**. The stuff you do once or twice (or more) a week, but not every day, should be on your Weekly Routine. This could be things like your Weekly Review, laundry, reviewing goals (although this could be put in your Weekly Review), house cleaning, exercise (if you exercise 3x a week, for example), errands, financial stuff, your Desk Day, gardening, yard work, etc.

  o Schedule these things throughout your week, trying not to pile too much on each day. You should have 2-3 things per day at the most. An ideal mix would be 1-2 things per day. If you have so many weekly tasks that you need 3-4 things per day, or more, you probably need to simplify, as it will be hard to maintain this schedule. Either batch some things together or eliminate the least important.

- **Trying it out**. Now that you've set your daily and weekly routines, give it a go. For the daily routines, try to stick with them for at least a week. At the end of the week, review how it went. If there are things that just didn't work, make adjustments. For the weekly routine, see if you can stick with it for at least two weeks (unless it's really not working, in which case you should adjust as you go along). Make adjustments, and try it again, until you find what works with you.

- **This is the trick — it's easy to set routines, but harder to stick with them**. But once you find a good set of routines that work for you, if you can stick with them for 30 days, it will become a habit. And you will find yourself feeling much calmer and in control of your life. How do you stick with it for 30 days? Make it a 30-day Challenge, give yourself rewards, commit to it in public, post your routines up on the wall at home and near your desk, and don't have any other goals or habit changes going on while you do this. If you can really put your energy and focus into it for 30 days, it will become more automatic and require less energy.

Chapter 14:
Habit 10: Find Your Passion

"Nothing great in the world has been accomplished without passion." Hegel

Of all the habits in Zen To Done, this one is the most difficult -- and yet, perhaps the most important.

If you do one thing in this book, this is the one I would recommend. Is it essential to the system? No. You could apply all the other habits, skip this one, and be productive, calm and organized. But this one step will make you not only much happier, but more productive.
Give it a thought: if you really want to do something, you'll work like hell to get it done. You'll work extra hard, you'll put in even more hours, and you're less likely to procrastinate. It's for work that you don't really care about that you procrastinate.

If you dread going to your job, or find yourself constantly lacking motivation, or find what you're doing dull and repetitive, you need to start looking for a new job. Staying in your current job will not only continue to make you unhappy, but you are not realizing your full potential in life.

Imagine this instead: you get up early, jumping out of bed, excited to go to work. You might put in more hours than the average person, but it doesn't seem difficult to you, because your work hours just zoom right by.

You are often in that state of mind often referred to as

"flow," where you can lose track of the world and time, losing yourself in the task at hand. Work is not work as many people refer to it, but something that is fun and interesting and exciting. It's not a "job" but a passion. If you've got a job you dislike, or even hate, this will sound like a

pipe dream to you. And if you never put in the effort to find what you're passionate about, you're right: such a thing will never be possible. But dare to dream, dare to imagine the possibilities, and dare to actually search for what you love, and it is not only a possibility, but a probability.

What do you really want to be doing right now? (Don't say sleeping!) What do you love doing? What is your dream job, and how can you get it? Give this some thought, not just right now but for the next few days. First you must identify that job, and then you'll have to plan how to get it.

How to Find Your Passion

What if you don't know what your passion is? Don't fret -- you're in the same boat as many people. The key is to start the search, and to keep looking until you find it.

Here are some suggestions:

- **Is there something you already love doing?** Do you have a hobby, or something you loved doing as a child, but never considered it as a possibility? Whether it's reading comic books, collecting something, making something, creating or building, there is probably a way you could do it for a living. Open a comic book shop, or create a comic book site online. If there's already something you love doing, you're ahead of the game. Now you just need to research the possibilities of making money from it.

- **What do you spend hours reading about?** For myself, when I get passionate about something, I'll read about it for hours on end. I'll buy books and magazines. I'll spend days on the Internet finding out more. There may be a few possibilities here for you and all of them are possible career paths. Don't close your mind to these topics. Look into them.

- **Brainstorm**. Nothing comes to mind right away? Well, get out a sheet of paper, and start writing down ideas. Anything that comes to mind, write it down. Look around your house, on your computer, on your bookshelf, for inspirations, and just write them down. There are no bad ideas at this stage. Write everything down, and evaluate them later.

- **Ask around, and surf for possibilities**. Ask other people for ideas. See what others have discovered as their passions. Look all over the Internet for ideas. The more possibilities you find, the more likely your chances of finding your true passion.

- **Give it a try first**. It's best to actually test your new idea before jumping into it as a career. Do it as a hobby or side job at first, so that you can see if it's really your true calling. You may be passionate about it for a few days, but where the rubber meets the road is whether you're passionate about it for at least a few months. If you pass this test, you have probably found it.

- **Never quit trying**. Can't find your passion at first? Give up after a few days and you're sure to fail. Keep trying, for months on end if necessary and you'll find it eventually. Thought you found your passion but you got tired of it? No problem! Start over again and find a new passion. There may be more than one passion in your lifetime, so explore all the possibilities. Found your passion but haven't been successful making a living at it? Don't give up. Keep trying, and try again, until you succeed. Success doesn't come easy, so giving up early is a sure way to fail. Keep trying, and you'll get there.

How to Get There

Once you've found your passion, you've taken a huge step towards happiness! Congratulations! Celebrate this fact, then roll up your sleeves, because you're not there yet.

Here are some suggestions for actually living your passion:

- **Don't quit your job just yet**. If you find your calling, your passion, don't just turn in your resignation tomorrow. It's best to stay in your job while you're researching the possibilities. If you can do your passion as a side job, and build up the income for a few months or a year, that's even better. It gives you a chance to build up some savings (and if you're going into business for yourself, you'll need that cash reserve), while practicing the skills you need.

- **Do some research**. Who else is doing your dream job? What is their experience? How did they get the job?

What are the requirements? Research it on the internet, ask people you know, make some calls. The more info you have, the better.

- **What are your obstacles?** What do you need to do to get there? Do you need an education? Do you need to know the right people? Do you just need to fill out an application? Do you need to learn some skills?

- **Make a plan**. Work out some solutions to your obstacles. If you need an education or skills, you will not be able to execute this plan overnight, but if you don't plan it out now, you might never get there. Lay out the path to your success.

- **Take action**. Don't wait for opportunity to come hit you on the head. Go out and grab that opportunity. Execute your plan — do at least one thing today, and each day, until you get there. It might seem like it will take forever, but if you really put in the work, you'll achieve your dreams someday.

- **Practice, and practice, and practice some more**. Don't go into it with amateur skill level. If you want to make money — to be a professional — you need to have professional skills.

- **Get very good at your future career** and you will make money at it. Practice for hours on end. If it's something you love, the practice should be something you want to do.

- **Be persistent**. Don't give up because you've been rejected a few times (or even a lot of times). Keep knocking on doors. Keep making those calls. Keep submitting your resume. Keep making appointments. Don't ever let up. The person who is relentless will win over the person who quits.

- Land your dream job, doing something that you're passionate about, and you may never need to motivate yourself to be productive again.

Chapter 15:
A Day with Zen to Done

" Never mistake motion for action." Ernest Hemingway

You might think about all of this, about the 10 habits, and wonder what it would look like in practice. Well, Zen To Done is pretty much the system I use, and I can tell you what a ZTD day would be like.

However, instead of getting into the details of my personal life, let's look at a hypothetical Zen To Doner ... just to give us an idea of what the system looks like in practice. We'll take a look at Steve, who has been implementing the habits of ZTD for the past year.

Morning

Steve's an early riser, so he gets up at 5:30 a.m. This is by no means mandatory in Zen To Done, of course, but Steve enjoys it. First thing to say about Steve in the morning? He's quick to get up, because he's excited about his day. Why? Because in the past year, he's achieved Habit 10, and found his passion. It's now his job, and he does it at home. Of course, you don't need to work at home to implement ZTD, but Steve enjoys it.

So he gets up out of bed, ready to greet the day. Then he begins his morning routine: he grooms himself, then enjoys a nice cup of coffee and watches the sunrise.

Then he begins his morning writing ritual, writing an article that also happens to be one of his Most Important

Tasks (MITs) for today.
When he's done, he changes to his running clothes, laces up his shoes, and goes for a 30-minute run. Steve enjoys his run, because it gives him some quiet time to think. After his run, he takes a quick shower, eats a healthy breakfast, and then gets to his second MIT for today.

When he does one of his MITs, Steve clears his desk, turns off the Internet and phone, closes all programs on the computer except the one he needs to do his work, and focuses completely on the task at hand. He will get up and take a break every 10-15 minutes, but doesn't allow himself to connect to email or other distractions, until he's done.

Only when he's completed this morning routine, and done two of his MITs, does he allow himself to check email and read his morning RSS feeds.

Planning

Steve actually set his three MITs the night before, during his evening routine, so he would be ready for the day. He uses a simple Moleskine pocket notebook as his ZTD tool, and on a fresh page, he puts the day's date, and then lists his three MITs for the day. At the bottom of the page, he lists his "batch tasks" -- smaller tasks that he has to do during the day, but that he saves up for "batch processing" later in the day so that they don't interrupt his MITs. He also uses the Moleskine notebook as a "capture" tool, carrying it wherever he goes, and has a section (marked by a little Post-it) where he writes down thoughts and tasks as they come to him.

Today also happens to be the day of his Simple Weekly

Review, so he does a quick run-through of his system, spending only 30 minutes on the review. He goes through his to-do list (which he keeps at the back of his Moleskine notebook), and weeds out tasks he doesn't really need to do, leaving only those that are most important.

He reviews his Single Goal for this year, ensuring that some of his Big Rocks for the next week are related to moving that Single Goal forward. He also looks at the progress he's made on that Single Goal in the last week, and is pleased that he's actually ahead of schedule. He crosses off some tasks that were completed, and then emails a few tasks to others that he doesn't really need to do himself. Satisfied that his list is simplified as far as possible, he now plans his Big Rocks for the coming week, ensures that his inboxes are empty and his filing system in place.

Evening Routine

Steve's day goes pretty much as planned. He accomplishes his three MITs, which is satisfying, and gets most of the batch tasks done near the end of the day. He clears out his email inbox and his physical inbox by the end of the day. A few other tasks came up, but he disposed of them quickly, adding one to his to-do list at the back of his notebook.

After he's cleared out his inboxes, finished his batch tasks, and checked off his lists, Steve does the rest of his evening routine. He gets lunches prepared for his kids for tomorrow morning, reviews his calendar and to-do list to see what he needs to do tomorrow, selecting his three MITs. He reviews his day, writing in a journal to record his progress and thoughts.

Chapter 16:
The ZTD FAQ

A number of readers have written to me with questions about Zen To Done, and I thought it would be useful to address them here in a Frequently Asked Questions format.

How is ZTD different from GTD? It seems the same.
Zen To Done adopts some of the principles of GTD and other productivity systems ... but with some different focuses:

1. GTD asks you to adopt a bunch of new habits all at once, and so many people have failed. As I've talked about on Zen Habits, habit changes require a lot of energy and focus to be successful, and it's much better to do one at a time. ZTD asks people to do the habits of GTD one at a time (or two at the most).

2. ZTD focuses on simplifying what you are going to do down to the essentials, and not trying to tackle everything. GTD has less of a focus on what's important, and instead treats everything coming in the same.

3. With GTD, many people have focused on the tools and the system, while ZTD focuses more on doing. It presents a way of doing your tasks so that you are focused on one task at a time, clearing your distractions, and getting into the zone. GTD doesn't talk much about the actual doing.

4. GTD only cursorily mentions goals. It is intentionally a bottom-up approach, and for what it tries to do, it is great. But ZTD focuses more on goals -- during your yearly, monthly, and weekly reviews, and on a daily basis with your

   MITs. So it combines the bottom-up approach of GTD with the top-down approach of people like Steven Covey.

5. With GTD, your day is very unstructured, which again is a strength, but for some people can be difficult and confusing. ZTD adds structure to your day with your MITs and with your routines (morning, evening and otherwise). Many people find this easier to work with, but it's an optional habit.

6. Finally, ZTD adds the last habit of finding your passion. While not strictly a task-related habit, finding your passion is extremely important in doing something you love, so that you actually get more done. I think this is an important point for a lot of people.

With Habit 8 (Simplify), aren't you defeating the purpose of GTD's mandate to get all open loops out of your head and dump them on your lists?

If you simplified before you wrote things in your capture tool (such as a pocket notebook), yes, that would defeat the purpose of the mandate to get things out of your head. However, ZTD asks you to first write them down, to get them out of your head, and then to review them later. It's during the review process that you simplify, and decide whether you really need to do the task, and whether it's really important.

This system doesn't seem very simple at all. It's 10 different habits! First, most productivity systems actually have way more than 10 habits. GTD has perhaps double that number, for example. Stephen Covey's 7 Habits are actually many more once you implement his entire system, where the rubber meets the road. For example, to implement the habit First Things First, you actually need to do several steps, putting things in quadrants, prioritizing from there, etc.

The other systems just don't spell out the habits as simply as ZTD does -- and they suggest you implement them all at once, which is a big reason for failure.

Second, you don't need to adopt all 10 habits. They are all good habits to adopt, but you can just choose 5 of them, for example. Use the habits that will help you the most, and will work with your working style. Everyone is different, and no one system will work for every single person. This approach allows flexibility.
For a more minimal approach, see Minimal ZTD in Chapter 3. It seems like it would take too much discipline to do only one habit at a time.

I agree, it can be difficult to restrain yourself enough to do one habit at a time. But it is actually much more difficult to try to adopt many habits at a time.

Think about it this way: what if you tried to quit smoking, become a runner, work out at the gym three times a week, become a vegetarian, wake up at 5 a.m. every day, stop procrastinating, become neat and organized, and do meditation ... all in the same week? How successful would you be? You'd probably fail, right?

The truth is, habit change is difficult. It's a skill that takes practice. It can definitely be done -- I've done it, and so have many others -- but it requires focus. You can't focus on 10 things at a time. You can focus on a few at a time, but if you focus on one thing at a time, your focus is much more concentrated. That makes you much more likely to be successful.

If you think you're pretty good at habit changes, I would suggest you try adopting 3-4 habits at first, but not all 10. Perhaps try Minimal ZTD, and then add on other habits 1-2 at a time after those first 4 habits have been adopted. Do them one month at a time, and gradually add more.

Look at it like this: bad habits weren't formed overnight, and good habits won't be formed overnight either. If you adopt one habit per month, by the end of a year, you will be a very productive, organized, and calm person! Isn't that a pretty good accomplishment for a year?

What if I can't find my passion? Should I still implement the other habits?

The 10th habit is optional, and you should still adopt as many of the other habits as you can (or as apply to your work style), even if you're not in a job you love. However, the key to the 10th habit is to keep your eyes open. At least begin the search, and always be on the lookout for opportunities or ideas that could lead to you living a life where your passion is your work.

Do I really have to just stick to one goal per year? I have

so many I want to focus on!

I know how you feel! But again, focus is the key to achieving anything, and you can't focus on 10 goals at a time.

I know this for a fact, because I started out 2007 with a long list of goals I wanted to achieve, and a lot of enthusiasm. Each week, I would plan out the action steps needed to move all those goals forward. It wasn't long before my enthusiasm waned -- it's just too hard to keep that energy going for so many goals at once.

Instead, I've adopted a new approach: tackle one goal at a time. Now, do you need to take an entire year to accomplish that goal? No. You can focus on one goal that can be done in a week, or a month, or 6 months. But just focus on that goal. When you've accomplished it, then choose another. In this way, by maintaining that high level of focus, you can achieve a lot in a year.

Isn't ZTD a trademark infringement on David Allen's GTD? No, actually. First of all, although I am heavily indebted to David Allen and other productivity systems, David Allen didn't invent the concept of collection or processing or review. These have been the tools of productivity gurus for decades. Allen just put them together in a great system that is very logical and comprehensive, and makes sense.

I've taken some of those tools he uses (and that have been used for decades) and combined them with other tools that have been used for decades. Concepts such as Big Rocks and MITs, that were used by Stephen Covey ... and others before him. Concepts like simplifying, that became popular in the 1970s. Concepts like finding your passion, that are centuries old.

Second, "Zen To Done" is not an infringement upon "Getting Things Done". They only share one word in common, to start with, and there is not a chance that anyone would get the two terms confused. Also, while "ZTD" might sound like "GTD", David Allen does not hold the trademark on all combinations of letters that rhyme with "GTD".

In truth, I am indebted to David Allen, and others, but this system is my own blend of very useful tools, and one that others have found useful as well.

So what is your ZTD setup?

Everyone's setup will be different, as you need to find the tools and setup that work for you. However, if you're interested, here's my setup:

- Moleskine pocket notebook, that I carry everywhere and use as a capture tool.

- In the notebook, I write my three MITs for the day, along with "batch tasks" at the bottom of the page. I write my master to-do list, along with separate lists for errands and calls and follow-ups, in the back of the notebook.

- I use Google Calendar for appointments only (and my kids' activities), Gmail for email, and Google Documents and AbiWord for writing.

That's all!

Resources

Tools

- To-do lists: Vitalist, Tadalist, Backpack, Simple GTD, Nozbe,
  Tracks, Remember the Milk.

- Calendars: Google Calendar, 30 Boxes.

- Others: Cool Timer, Hipster PDA.

Articles

- MITs
- Big Rocks
- Clearing Your Email Inbox
- Clearing Your Desk
- Morning Routine
- Evening Routine
- 30 Day Challenge
- Top 20 Motivation Hacks
- Executing Your To-do List
- Weekly Review
- GTD FAQ
- Massive GTD Resources List

Forms

In the next few pages, some sample forms are provided:
- Single Goal Form
- ZTD Weekly Form
- ZTD Daily Form
- ZTD Lists

ZEN TO DONE FORMS

Single Goal Form

2007	
This Year's Single Goal:	
Mantra for Single Goal (2-4 words):	
First sub goal (1-2 weeks):	

Note: After accomplishing the first sub-goal, check it off and create a second sub-goal, and so on, until Single Goal is accomplished. Each sub-goal should take about 1-2 weeks to accomplish, but can be a little more or less if needed.

ZEN TO DONE FORMS

Weekly Forms

Week of	
Mantra:	
Current Single Goal sub-goal:	
Big Rock #1:	
Big Rock #2:	
Big Rock #3:	
Big Rock #4:	
Big Rock #5:	

Projects this week	

ZEN TO DONE FORMS

Weekly Forms

Simple Weekly Review Checklist
Review Single Goal for Year
Review short-term sub-goal for last week
Review notes
Review calendar
Review context lists
Review someday/maybe, follow-up, project lists
Plan short-term sub-goal for this week
Plan Big Rocks for this week

Weekly Routine
Monday:
Tuesday:
Wednesday:
Thursday:
Friday:
Saturday:
Sunday:

ZEN TO DONE FORMS
Lists

Projects List	Personal Tasks	Calls

Work Tasks	Follow-up	Errands

Someday

Thank you to my wife, Eva, for the patience in allowing me to write this book, and for everything else you've done.

Thank you to James Wondrack (wondrackdesign.com) for the excellent design at an extremely low cost -- perfect for a cheapskate like me. He met my minimalist standards and exceeded them with his great taste.

And most of all, thank you to the readers of Zen Habits, who have encouraged me in more ways than they know.

Leo

The Only Guide to Happiness You'll Ever Need

"The Constitution only guarantees the American people the right to pursue happiness. You have to catch it yourself." - *Benjamin Franklin*

For some of us, the ultimate goal in life is happiness. Whether we see fulfillment in our work, contentment in our relationships, passion in our hobbies … we strive to find happiness.

"Happiness is the meaning and the purpose of life, the whole aim and end of human existence." – *Aristotle*

And yet, this search for happiness can be a lifelong search, especially if we look at happiness as something that will come once we achieve certain goals — a nice home, a perfect spouse, the ultimate promotion … and when we get these goals, instead of being happy, we often are looking forward to being happy when we meet our next goals.

Happiness shouldn't be something that happens to us in the future, maybe someday, if things go well. Happiness should be here and now, who we are now, with the people we're with now, doing the things we're doing now. And if we're not with people who make us happy, and doing things that make us happy … then we should take action to make that happen.

That's the simple formula for happiness. Take action to do the things that make you happy, with the people who make you happy, and to be happy with the person you are now. (**Disclaimer**: this probably doesn't apply, of course, to those who are clinically depressed or who have other similar medical conditions which I am not qualified to discuss.)

Don't wait for happiness. Seize it.
"If you want to be happy, be." - *Leo Tolstoy*

Here's how — a list of action you can take today to seize that happiness. You don't have to do these all at once, but you should do most (if not all) of them eventually, and sooner rather than later. Pick one or two and start today.

1. **Be present**. Don't think about how great things will be in the future. Don't dwell on what did or didn't happen in the past. Learn to be in the here and now, and experience life as it's happening, and appreciate the world for the beauty that it is, right now. Practice makes perfect with this crucial skill.

2. **Connect with others**. In my experience, very few things can achieve happiness as well as connecting with other human beings, cultivating relationships, bonding with others.

3. **Spend time with those you love**. This might seem almost the same as the item above, and in reality it's an extension of the same concept, a more specific application. Spending time with the people you love is extremely important to happiness … and yet it's incredible how often we do just the opposite, and spend time alone, or disconnected from those we love, or spend time with people we don't much like. *Make it a priority* to schedule time with the people you love.

Make that your most important item of the day. For myself, I have a time when I cut off work, and the rest of the day is for my family. Weekends are exclusively for my family. And by setting aside this sacred time, I ensure my happiness by letting nothing come between me and the people I love most.

4. **Do the things you love**. What do you love doing most? Figure out the 4-5 things you love doing most in life, the things that make you happiest, and make those the foundation of your day, every day. Eliminate as much of the rest as possible. For me, the things I love doing are: spending time with my family, writing, reading, and running. I do those things every day, and very little else. It may take awhile to get your life down to your essentials like I have (it took me a few years of careful elimination and rescheduling and saying "no" to requests that aren't on my short list), but it's worth the effort.

5. **Focus on the good things**. Everyone's life has positive and negative aspects — whether you're happy or not depends largely on which aspects you focus on. Did you lose today's softball game? At least you got to spend time with friends doing something fun. Did you sprain your ankle running? Well, your body probably needed a week's rest anyway, as you were running too much! Did your baby get sick? Well, at least it's only a flu virus and nothing life-threatening … and at least you have a wonderful baby to nurse to health! You can see my point — almost everything has a positive side, and focusing on the positives make all the difference. My Auntie Kerry died last week (as you know), and I'm still grieving, but 1) I'm happy I spent time with her before her death; 2) her death has brought our

family closer together; 3) her suffering has ended; and 4) it reminded me to spend more time with the people I love while they're still alive.

6. **Do work you love**. An extension, of course, of doing the things you love, but applied to work. Are you already doing the work you love? Then you're one of the lucky ones, and you should appreciate how lucky you are. If you aren't doing the work you love, you should make it a priority to try to find work you're passionate about, and to steer your career in that direction. Take myself for example: I was doing work that I was good at (just last year), but that I wasn't passionate about. I was passionate about writing, and so I pursued blogging … and with a year of hard work, was able to quit my day job and blog full time. I'm so much happier these days!

7. **Lose yourself in your work**. Once you've found work you love, the key is to lose yourself in it … clear away all distractions, find an interesting and challenging task, and just pour all your energy and focus into that task. With practice, you'll forget about the outside world. There are few work-related joys that equal this feeling.

8. **Help others**. Is there any better feeling than helping a fellow human being? There aren't many. And it's not too hard.

9. **Find time for peace**. With the hectic pace of life these days, it's hard to find a moment of peace. But if you can make time for solitude and quiet, it can be one of the happiest parts of your day.

10. **Notice the small things**. Instead of waiting for the big things to happen — marriage, kids, house, nice car, big promotion, winning the lottery — find happiness in the small things that happen every day. Little things like having a quiet cup of coffee in the early morning hours, or the delicious and simple taste of berries, or the pleasure of reading a book with your child, or taking a walk with your partner. Noticing these small pleasures, throughout your day, makes a huge difference.

11. **Develop compassion**. Compassion is developing a sense of shared suffering with others … and taking steps to alleviate the suffering of others. I think too often we forget about the suffering of others while focusing on our own suffering, and if we learned to share the suffering of others, our suffering would seem insignificant as a result. Compassion is an extremely valuable skill to learn, and you get better with practice.

12. **Be grateful**. Learning to be grateful for what's in our lives, for the people who have enriched our lives, goes a long way toward happiness. It helps us to appreciate what we have and what we have received, and the people who have helped us.

13. **Become a lifelong learner**. I find an inordinate amount of pleasure in reading, in learning about new things, in enriching my knowledge as I get older. I think spending time reading some of the classics, as well as passionately pursuing new interests, is energy well invested. Try to do a little of it every day, and see if it doesn't make you happier.

14. **Simplify your life**. This is really about identifying the

things you love (see above) and then eliminating everything else as much as possible. By simplifying your life in this way, you create time for your happiness, and you reduce the stress and chaos in your life. In my experience, living a very simple life is also a pleasure in itself.

15. **Slow down**. Similar to simplifying, slowing down is just a matter of reminding yourself that there's no need to rush through life. Schedule less things on your calendar, and more space between things. Learn to eat slower, drive slower, walk slower (unless you're doing it for exercise). Going slowly helps to reduce stress, and improve the pleasure of doing things, and keeps you in the present moment.

16. **Exercise**. I've written about the pleasures of exercise many times. It can be hard to start an exercise program but once you get going, it relieves stress and can really give you a good feeling. I feel joyful every time I go out for a run!

17. **Meditate**. You don't need to join a Zendo or get a mat or learn any lotus positions, but the simplest form of meditation can really help you to be present and to get out of the worrying part of your head. You can do it right now: close your eyes and simply try to focus on your breathing as long as possible. Pay attention to the breath as it comes into your body, and then as it goes out. When you feel your mind start to wander, don't fret, but just simply acknowledge the other thoughts, and then return to your breathing. Do this a little each day and you'll get better at it.

18. **Learn to accept**. One of the challenges for people like

me — people who want to improve themselves and change the world — is learning to accept things as they are. Sometimes it's better to learn to accept, and to love, the world as it is, and people as they are, rather than to try to make everything and everyone conform to an impossible ideal. I'm not saying you should accept cruelty and injustice, but learn to love things when they are less than "perfect".

19. **Spend time in nature**. Go outside and take a walk each day, or take the time to watch a sunset or sunrise. Or find a body of water — the ocean, a lake, a river, a pond — and spend time taking a look at it, contemplating it. If you're lucky enough to live near some woods, or a mountain, or a canyon, go hiking. Time in nature is time invested in your happiness.

20. **Find the miracles in life**. I absolutely believe in miracles, and believe that they are all around us, every day. My children are all miracles. The kindnesses of strangers are miracles. The life growing all around us is a miracle. Find those miracles in your life, and enjoy the majesty of them.

The Getting Things Done (GTD) FAQ

I get a lot of email about Getting Things Done (GTD), mostly from people just starting out who have various questions about implementation, starting out, or sticking to the system. I thought I'd start a FAQ to help those with similar questions.

Now, let me first say that this is not a complete FAQ, but I've taken some of the most common questions. I'd like you guys to help out by submitting other questions that I can add to the list when I update it.

Let me also say that I am not the absolute authority on GTD — I am but one blogger, one practitioner, and I am just sharing what I've learned from experience and reading other sites. But I hope it's of some use!

Overview

What is GTD?

The official answer is given by David Allen, the author of Getting Things Done on his website, www.davidco.com. The full answer is here: http://www.davidco.com/what_is_gtd.php but here's the most important snippet:

GTD embodies an easy, step-by-step and highly efficient method for achieving this relaxed , productive state. It includes:

- Capturing anything and everything that has your attention

- Defining actionable things discretely into outcomes and concrete next steps

- Organizing reminders and information in the most streamlined way, in appropriate categories, based on how and when you need to access them.

- Keeping current and "on your game" with appropriately frequent reviews of the six horizons of your commitments (purpose, vision, goals, areas of focus, projects, and actions)

- Implementing GTD alleviates the feeling of overwhelm, instills confidence, and releases a flood of creative energy. It provides structure without constraint, managing details with maximum flexibility.

How do I start?

Well, the book gives you a step-by-step approach, but the most important steps for starting out are:

Processing all the papers in your desk and inbox to empty.

Processing your email and other inboxes to empty.

Capturing all tasks and ideas on a notebook or mobile device.

Setting up an easy reference filing system.

Creating context lists for all of your actions, along with a project list, a Waiting For list and a Someday/Maybe list.

Using a calendar or tickler file to remind you of future tasks or appointments.

Doing a Weekly Review to keep the system together.

How long will it take to start?

Well, the longest part for many people is processing all the papers on their desks and elsewhere and getting all their inboxes to zero. This can take anywhere from a few hours to a day or three. Next longest is setting up a filing system and your lists. That can take an hour or two. The other stuff doesn't take setup time, usually. So altogether, you could be looking at a day or two (or more if your life is super disorganized). David Allen recommends you set aside a big chunk of your time for a day or two to clear everything off and get it set up.
Now, although this sounds like a big commitment (and it is), I have to say that it is worth it. This step alone is worth the price of the GTD book — getting everything cleared and organized is a huge accomplishment and an amazing feeling. It's why so many people love GTD.

Is there an easier way to start?

Yes. You don't need to implement all of GTD at once. Really, you should go with what works for you — there is no one way to do it. A minimal starting point could be any of the following:

- **Just start with capture.** All you need is a notebook and a pen, and start writing everything down, so you never forget stuff again, and you get it out of your head. If you feel like doing more, use the notebook to create some context lists — your next actions (see below) organized into the contexts in which you do them (work, home, errands, calls, etc.) so you can just look at the actions you can do right now.

- **Clear out your inbox**. The next step, if you're ready, would be to process all your papers. Gather them in one pile, and work from top to bottom, disposing of each one until you're done. This is an amazing feeling. From here on out, get an inbox, and use it as your one point of entry for all papers (including Post-its and phone messages and receipts and everything else). If you're feeling ambitious, take the next step and do the same with your email inbox.

- **Filing**. A simple start could also include a simple filing system. All you need is a filing cabinet (or a drawer dedicated to your filing needs if that's all you need), some manila folders and some labels. Have plenty of them on hand so you can create a folder quickly and easily. Use a simple alphabetical system.

I'm overwhelmed by my inbox and all the stuff I need to sort through!

This can be very overwhelming, especially if you've got large piles of paper scattered all over your desk and in drawers and on the floor and in the car, etc. But it's doable. First of all, gather them all up and put them in one pile. If it's too huge to put in one pile, make two, but don't start creating a whole bunch of piles. The key is to start at the top of the pile and work your way down, one document at a time, so if you have two piles, consider the second pile just a continuation of the first.

Next, if you don't have time to process through all of them at once (and you should try if you can), then just set aside the pile for now and process it in chunks. I would recommend setting aside an hour a day to process your pile. Again, start from the top, and dispose of each document. When you get to the bottom, buy yourself a treat!

Is GTD a cult? Why is it so popular on the Internet?

GTD is often accused of having a cult-like status, but in truth it just inspires a lot of passion. Why? First of all, because of the feeling of getting your desk cleared and your inboxes to empty. Seriously, as I said above, this is an amazing, awesome feeling. Second, because of the simple power of concepts like next actions, context lists and the weekly review — they are not anything complicated, but they work extremely well, and people love that.

Third, because of the open-source nature of the tools — this is what gets so many geeks. They love being able to use their favorite gadget, or computer program, or show off their programming skills by just using an automated text file, or the textile feeling of a good pen on good paper. It's all about individual pleasures, and setting up your cool tools to create a setup that works for you. It's the geek in us that loves GTD.

Tools

What tools do I need?

As mentioned above, a minimal setup would include a

notebook, pen, inbox, filing drawer, folders and labels. However, there are many other tools you could use, including but not limited to:

- a mobile device such as a PDA for everything - capture, lists, reminders an electronic labeler for neat labels a calendar or calendar program (highly recommended)

- computer software (off-line or online) to handle your lists or your capture

- a tickler file, either using folders (see next question) or software

- index cards for capture and lists

What is a tickler file or 43 folders, and do I need it?

A tickler file, as spelled out in the book, is a system of 43 folders: 12 folders labeled for each month, and 31 folders labeled for the days of the month. So the way it works:

- If you have a piece of paper (or a concert ticket, etc.) that you don't need to think about until later this month, put it in one of the daily folders (let's say the folder labeled "20″ if we want to look at it on the 20th of this month).

- If you don't need to think about it until a later month, put it in that month's folder.

- Each day, you look in the folder with today's date on it (if today is the 20th, I'll look in "20″) and see what you need to think about today. If you want to postpone it until later, simply put the paper in a later folder. In this way, you could have a recurring reminder. Each day, the folder with today's date should be at the front of the pile — rotate yesterday's folder to the back of the pile.

- At the end of each month, rotate the past month's folder to the back of the month folders pile, and look in the next month's folder — take out the papers in it and redistribute throughout the 31 day folders.

It's an ingenious system, and if it appeals to you, give it a try. However, many people (myself included) find this system a bit cumbersome, especially given the ease-of-use of today's computer calendars (I use Gcal). Using a calendar program, you could just mark a reminder on the date in the calendar. You can even set up recurring reminders.

Hi-tech vs. lo-tech?

This is the real question for GTD users when it comes to tools: do you go with a paper system (such as the Moleskine, the Hipster PDA, the PocketMod, etc.) or with a digital system ... or as many people do, a combination of both. Of course the answer is that it's a highly personal question, and you should go with the tools that work for you — and especially the tools you love to use. If that's a PDA, then go for it. If that's a Moleskine, that's great too. Usually it takes a little bit of experimentation to find the right tools — however, I would caution against obsessing over tools, as this is the biggest waste of time for most GTDers — pick your tools, and go with them. Focus more on actually doing your tasks than what cool tools you're going to use.

You'd think that geeks on the Internet would go with digital tools, especially online ones or with PDAs or smart phones. And many do. However, there is a large number of geeks (myself included) who end up using analog (paper) tools such as the ones mentioned above. Why? That's an often debated topic, but the reasons usually have to do with simplicity, ease of use, portability, ease of expansion and modification, and especially the tactile pleasure of using paper and a good pen. Ultimately, it's something you'll have to choose for yourself.

What's the best GTD software?

There are so many out there, it would be impossible to choose just one. And it really depends on your needs and personal preferences. A couple of things to read:

Wikipedia's Comparison of GTD software
http://en.wikipedia.org/wiki/Comparison_of_GTD_softwa
re

5 Simple, Effective GTD Tools
http://zenhabits.net/2007/05/5-simple-effective-gtd-tools/

I'm stuck with Outlook at work. Can I set up Outlook for GTD?

Absolutely — many people have. I would recommend reading

Davidco's GTD and Outlook:

http://www.davidco.com/store/catalog/GTD-and-Outlook-p-16173.php

What about implementing GTD on a Mac?

The Mac is a great GTD tool. 43Folders blog (www.43folders.com) is an excellent source for more information, or see this MeFi thread for some good stuff:

Ask Metafilter: Getting Things Done on a Macintosh:

http://ask.metafilter.com/18937/Getting-Things-Done-on-a-Macintosh

Is it OK to have multiple setups on my computer, PDA, and planner?

Again, what works best for you is what you should go with. But my recommendation? Simplify. It's hard to continually check and update different lists and calendars on a computer, a PDA and a paper planner. You are more likely to use and stick with the system if you just have one place to check and update. Find the one that works best for you and stick with it.

Next Actions, Contexts, Projects

Next actions - what are they?

Basically, for any project (and a project is anything that takes more than 1 action), you need to ask yourself, "What is the very next physical action necessary to move this project forward?" It is this "next action" that you put on your to-do list. The problem with many tasks that we put on our to-do lists is that they are not really something you can do, but a mini-project. For example, "Write report" is a project where the next action might be "Look on Internet for three sources for report" or "Call Larry to get stats for report".

I have too many next actions (or projects) — what should I do?

It's true that having a long list of next actions can be overwhelming for many people. Note: this advice also applies to too many projects. There are a few ways to deal with this:

- Realize that you don't need to do all of these next actions today or even over the next few days. It's just good to know all of your commitments, instead of having them pop into your brain over and over at the wrong times.

- If this list cannot be accomplished this week, move the less urgent ones to your Someday/Maybe list and just leave the ones you intend to accomplish this week. Then, in your Weekly Review, move those tasks you can accomplish next week back up to the current context lists.

- Simplify — eliminate or delegate those tasks that aren't really essential, or that no longer need to be done.

- Crank out as many of the smaller tasks as possible, to shorten the list. You'll still never clear your list, but you can make it more manageable.

A few next actions seem to hang around on my lists.

Suggestions?

If you have some stubborn next actions that stay on your lists for a long time, you should take a look at them in your Weekly Review. Why are these actions so hard to remove from your lists? Here are a few suggestions:

- Perhaps you don't want to do them — in that case, do them first thing in the morning, before you check email, and don't do anything until those tasks are done.

- Or perhaps you don't need to do them — if they've been on your list a few weeks, they probably aren't that urgent. See if you can eliminate them or delegate them.

- Perhaps they aren't really next actions. Often there are projects on our list that are disguised as actions. See if the task actually involves more than one step (for example, "Call Larry" might actually be, "Call Nina to get Larry's number"), and then put the real next action on your list instead.

- Perhaps the tasks are too intimidating. In that case, break them down to smaller tasks. "Write Report" could be "Write first paragraph of report" or "Outline report" or "Write report for 10 minutes".

- If it turns out this is something you need to do, but perhaps not right now, move it to your Someday/Maybe list.

How granular should a next action be?

When a next action is intimidating, as I suggested in the

previous question, you can break it down to a smaller level ("granularize it"). But how small do you break it down? That's really a personal preference — do you work better in 30 minute chunks, 2 hour chunks, or 10 minute chunks? Give it a little thought and experiment.

Some ideas to try:

- Do the next action — write the report until you are done, or until you need a break.

- Use a time chunk — again, the amount of the chunk depends on you, but it should be something you can do without taking a break. If you can work 2 hours without a break, in one burst, then that should be your level. If you can only work 10 minutes before needing a breather, that's your level.

- Try a small unit — 5 pages, or 2 things on the outline, or 50 lines of code.

Try a larger unit - a chapter of a novel, for example.

How many next actions for one project should be on my lists?

If you've got a project that consists of multiple physical actions, how many of those actions should you write on your list? The answer is at least one — every active project should have at least one next action on an active context list. If you'd like to put more, that's really up to you, but be aware that having all of your project's actions on your context lists can be intimidating and overwhelming.

My recommendation is to go with one or two at the most. And if you have 2-3 next actions from a project listed on your context lists, be sure that each of them can be accomplished without something else being done first. For example, don't put "Mail letter" and "Buy stamps" on your list, as you cannot do the first without first doing the second. The first action ("Mail letter") is known as a dependent action — you can't do it without doing something else first. Don't list dependent actions on your context lists, as it wastes your time to look at actions you can't actually do.

When you've completed a project's next action, don't just check it off. Be sure to write the project's next "next action" on your list, so the project continues to move forward. If you forget, that's OK — during your Weekly Review, one of the most important parts of the process is making sure that each project on your projects list has a next action listed on your context lists.

How do I handle every day or every week actions?

If you have tasks that recur every day or every week (let's say laundry, or a daily report), there are a number of ways to handle this:

- Put it in your calendar or tickler file as a recurring task. Every day (or every week, or however often the task needs to be done), you should see it in your calendar, and note it on your list as something that needs to be done today.

- Today list — this is not actually a part of GTD, but if you want, you can have a Today list where you

101

note the things that need to be done today — such as your daily report, or one of your Most Important Tasks (MITs). Don't put anything that doesn't absolutely need to be done today on your Today list, or it will become useless. I suggest only having three things on this list.

- Context list — you could just put the task at the top of the appropriate context list, and then every day, when you check your context list, you'll see it there.

- Routines — this is also not explicitly a part of GTD, but you could create a separate list for Daily Routines and Weekly Routines where you make sure to check off items each day or each week. Actually, GTD allows for other lists, such as checklists, so this could technically be a part of GTD.

What contexts should I use?

This is a highly personal choice, and also takes experimentation to get it right. The main idea is to group your next actions so that when you look at a context list, you are only looking at tasks that can actually be done right now, in the location you're in with the tools you have. So if you look at your Home list, it should not contain items that can only be done from your work computer. Similarly, your Work list should not contain your errands that can only be done on the road. You can further break down a context such as Work if there are different contexts at work. For example, if you use different work locations, and some tasks can only be done at one of the locations. In that case, you should not be looking at those tasks if you're in the other location where the tasks can't be done. If you start to notice that there are next actions on your context list that you cannot actually do right now, that is either because 1) your contexts need to be re-examined; 2) the task is not actually a next action but a dependent task or project; or 3) the next action belongs on your Someday/Maybe list.

Sticking To It

I have trouble sticking to my Weekly Review. Any suggestions?

This is a toughie for most GTDers (including myself). It's best to analyze why you're having trouble, and address the reason. Here are some suggestions:

- If the weekly review is taking too long, shorten it by processing your inboxes to empty the day before, and making sure your process for the review is streamlined.

- If you find that you get too busy and keep pushing the Weekly Review back, try first thing in the morning on Monday. Schedule an appointment for two hours, and don't let anything interrupt it.

- If that doesn't work, do it on Sunday afternoon, when you have more time.

- Reward yourself for completing it. Actually, completing the Weekly Review is in itself a reward, because it's nice to get your system organized, so remind yourself of that. But also give yourself an external reward.

Help! I've fallen off GTD and I can't get back on.

This happens all the time — people get gung-ho about GTD and then a couple months later something comes up that gets them too busy to keep the system organized, and it falls apart. Luckily, GTD is super easy to get back into — in fact it's easier to get back into it than it is to get started in the first place, because you already know the system and you probably still have all the right tools — it's just a matter of setting yourself up and getting updated. It's actually fun to start again.

Some suggestions:

- **Try some cool tools** that you love to use. For me, that's the Moleskine notebook, as it is just a pleasure to use. For others, that might be a PDA or a cool online app. The tools you use are important, as they make you want to use the system. However, don't obsess over them.

- **Keep it simple**. Many people make complicated systems that are hard to hold together. Start simple, perhaps with paper tools or the simplest online tools, and don't get overboard.

- **Try with a minimal version** (see the top of this FAQ for more). You don't need to start full blast — just do a few things and then add later if necessary. You may find that the minimal version is all you need.

How do you stick with it once you get started again? See the next question.

I have trouble sticking with GTD.

How do you stick with GTD if you keep falling off it? Try these suggestions:

- **Weekly Review**. The key to sticking with GTD is the Weekly Review. Keep it short and simple, but be committed to it. If you only start with a minimal system, be sure to still do the Weekly Review. It keeps your system up to date, even if you get too busy to keep it up to date throughout the week.

- **Habits**. GTD is actually a series of habits (see Zen to Done for more), and the problem is that we try to adopt them all at once. If you've been reading Zen Habits for awhile, you know that you're more likely to be successful if you try to adopt one habit at a time. Try that with GTD — just do one habit first, then the next, and so on. You are much, much more likely to make GTD a habit as a whole and stick with it using this method.

- **Start small**. Instead of doing the whole system at once, try a minimal version (see the top of this FAQ for more). The minimal version is much less hassle to maintain, and therefore you're more likely to use it and stick with it. Keep it simple.

- **Tools you love**. Again, using tools you love make it more likely that you'll actually use them, and therefore stick with the system. Again, don't obsess over the tools, but pick ones that have a great appeal to you.

- **Online forum**. A good way to stick with anyone is to find a group that's doing the same thing. Try these forums to help you stick with it:

The 43Folders Google Group:
http://groups-beta.google.com/group/43Folders/

The David Allen Company public discussion board
http://www.davidco.com/forum/

GTD and Palm Pilot Yahoo Group
http://groups.yahoo.com/group/gtd_palm/

GTD Yahoo Group
http://finance.groups.yahoo.com/group/Getting_Things_Done/

GTD Tips & Techniques Google Group
http://groups.google.com/group/GTD-Tips--Techniques/about